Love and Logic® Money-isms

Wise Words About Raising Money-Smart Kids

800-338-4065 · www.loveandlogic.com

Wise words adapted from:

Millionaire Babies or Bankrupt Brats?
Love and Logic® Solutions to Teaching Kids About Money

by Jim Fay & Kristan Leatherman

The Love and Logic Press, Inc.
2207 Jackson Street, Golden, CO 80401-2300
www.loveandlogic.com
800-338-4065

LOVE AND LOGIC, LOVE & LOGIC, BECOMING A LOVE AND LOGIC PARENT, AMERICA'S PARENTING EXPERTS, LOVE AND LOGIC MAGIC, 9 ESSENTIAL SKILLS FOR THE LOVE AND LOGIC CLASSROOM, and 🔒 are registered trademarks or trademarks of the Institute For Professional Development, Ltd. and may not be used without written permission expressly granted from the Institute For Professional Development, Ltd.

Library of Congress Cataloging-in-Publication Data

Fay, Jim.
  Love and logic money-isms : wise words about raising money-smart kids / by Jim Fay & Kristan Leatherman.
      p. cm.
  "Wise words adapted from Millionaire babies or bankrupt brats? : love and logic solutions to teaching kids about money."
  ISBN 978-1-935326-01-4 (pbk.)
  1. Children--Finance, Personal. 2. Teenagers--Finance, Personal. 3. Child rearing--Economic aspects. I. Leatherman, Kristan. II. Fay, Jim. Millionaire babies or bankrupt brats? III. Title.
  HG179.F3748 2009
  332.0240083--dc22

                        2009019301

Project Coordinator: Kelly Borden
Editing by Jason Cook, Denver, CO
Cover and interior design by Michael Snell, Shade of the Cottonwood, Lawrence, KS
Illustration by Steve Ferchaud, Paradise, CA

Published and printed in the United States of America

*Dedicated to raising children
who have all that it takes
to make their dreams come true.*

Preface

If you are familiar with Love and Logic® you will enjoy this unique application of the philosophy developed by Jim Fay, Charles Fay, Ph.D., and Foster W. Cline, M.D.

If you are new to Love and Logic and wish to learn more, there are many resources offered through the Love and Logic Institute. Each of these books, articles, audios, etc. will give you practical, easy to learn techniques that solve many of the perplexing family issues that crop up in our daily lives.

This book shows how to apply Love and Logic to help kids learn about money. Each of the statements may leave you wanting to know more. As a way of providing more in-depth information on each of these ideas, we have included a reference at the bottom of each page.

Introduction

Love and Logic® Money–isms is a collection of wise words that capture the powerful and inspiring truths found in *Millionaire Babies or Bankrupt Brats? Love and Logic® Solutions to Teaching Kids About Money.*

If you would like to know how to set limits without losing your children's love, how to do what's best for your kids without feeling guilty, and how to do what's right in the short term to prevent future financial problems in the long term, this book is for you!

To better understand how to put these powerful insights into practice, *Money-isms* provides cross-references to Love and Logic's companion book on teaching kids about money: *Millionaire Babies or Bankrupt Brats?* Additional guidelines are footnoted as indicated by the icon:

May these insights touch your heart and mind, and contribute to a richer, better life with your children.

— Jim Fay & Kristan Leatherman

What is Love and Logic®?

Love and Logic is a menu of practical techniques designed to develop responsibility and increase the parent-child bond while preparing kids to make the decisions they will encounter in their adult lives.

The Love and Logic Process—The Four C's

- Share Control: Gain control by giving away the control you don't need.
- Share thinking and decision making: Provide opportunities for the child to do the greatest amount of thinking and decision making through Choices.
- Provide Consequences with empathy: An absence of anger causes the child to think and learn from their mistakes.
- Maintain the child's self-Concept: Increased self-concept leads to improved behavior, motivation, and achievement.

For more information about how to use Love and Logic's guiding principles check out these great books, *Parenting With Love and Logic* or *Parenting Teens With Love and Logic*.

While we wish it were different,

no one is granted immunity

from the consequences

of managing money unwisely.

See the story of Jack in "From Baby Shoes to Nursing Home Blues" on page 6.

Parents who share their financial stories,

both triumphs and failures,

raise kids who learn about the day-to-day

relationship between money and life.

MILLIONAIRE BABIES OR BANKRUPT BRATS?

For the top three "Reasons to Make Money Matter," see page 12.

Wise parents don't wait

for the schools to teach their children

practical money skills.

For a look at "Who's Filling the Fiscal Education Gap?," see page 15.

If we give pencils to children

to learn how to write,

and books to learn how to read,

then it makes sense to give them

their own money to learn how

to spend and save.

MILLIONAIRE BABIES OR BANKRUPT BRATS?

For a look at giving kids firsthand experience with money, see "Allowance Vows" on page 60.

Kids are ready for allowance

when they realize that money

can buy them the things they want,

and that their parents have

all the money.

MILLIONAIRE
BABIES
OR
BANKRUPT
BRATS?

For a look at allowance readiness, see the story of Freddie in "When Should I Start?" on page 64.

Wise parents give allowance

when they can afford it,

and model restraint when their

financial circumstances change.

MILLIONAIRE BABIES OR BANKRUPT BRATS?

To present allowance as part of a bigger family finance picture, see "When Allowance Doesn't Allow" on page 26, and "The Family Budget" page 199.

You know you're making progress

teaching your kids about the

real value of money when they

don't let you forget their allowance.

MILLIONAIRE BABIES OR BANKRUPT BRATS?

For guidelines on how much allowance and how often, see pages 61 and 66.

Kids learn faster about how to

make their allowance work

when parents have minimal rules

about its use.

For how to introduce allowance to your children, see "Rules or No Rules?" on page 72.

Wise parents use allowance
to give their kids lots of opportunities
to practice, and lots of opportunities
to make mistakes, while the price tags
are affordable.

See "Affordable vs. Unaffordable Mistakes" on page 24.

Kids learn more from

experiencing the consequences

than from hearing about them.

MILLIONAIRE BABIES OR BANKRUPT BRATS?

For how to set up monetary consequences, see "Kid-Sized Bills" on page 78.

When allowance gets lost or squandered,

wise parents remember to say with empathy,

"This is so sad. I give allowance once a week.

You'll get more on Saturday."

MILLIONAIRE BABIES OR BANKRUPT BRATS?

See the story of Dillon in "How to Make Forgetfulness Pay" on page 83, and "But I lost iiittt!" on page 71.

Wise parents introduce

the abstract world of plastic "money" cards

long after their kids have had lots of

concrete success with cash and coins.

MILLIONAIRE BABIES OR BANKRUPT BRATS?

For ideas about the best way to introduce money to your children, see "Paper or Plastic?" on page 88.

A debit card in the hands of

an irresponsible kid is not an asset

to the kid, but a menu for disaster.

See "Prepaid, Debit, or Credit Cards?" on page 90.

MILLIONAIRE
BABIES
OR
BANKRUPT
BRATS?

Giving a child a credit card

doesn't teach responsibility.

Giving them a chance to earn one

by demonstrating maturity and

responsibility does.

MILLIONAIRE
BABIES
OR
BANKRUPT
BRATS?

See "Credit Cards" on page 93, and "Credit Card Tips: When the Time Comes" on page 94.

Chores are the basic building blocks

for feeling loved, valued and needed

by one's family. Kids who get this at home

don't go looking for it in a cult

or street gang.

See "Gillian's Story: A Mini–Me, Me, Me!" on page 100.

Don't expect a teacher to be able

to motivate your children to pick up a pencil

at school if they are not required

to lift a finger at home.

Chores at home are the cornerstone

of achievement at school.

MILLIONAIRE BABIES OR BANKRUPT BRATS?

See "What's School Got to Do with Chores?" on page 40.

Wise parents don't pay their kids

for completing chores.

MILLIONAIRE BABIES OR BANKRUPT BRATS? See "Three Reasons Why Allowance Tied to Chores Is Ineffective" on page 27, and "Stars, Hearts, and Sticker Charts" on page 104.

Despite complaints that "it's not fair"

and comparisons to the "easier" lives

of their kid's friends, wise parents don't deny

their kids the opportunity to contribute

to the welfare of the family through chores.

For how to introduce kids to a chore list, see page 106.

Wise parents know that the secret ingredient

to reducing power struggles

is to give kids

a day-to-day menu of choices.

See "Contributions by Choice" on page 115, and "Love and Logic Guidelines for Giving Effective Choices" on page 35.

There's nothing wrong with a child

that an arguing parent can't make worse.

Wise parents don't dignify the ridiculous

by offering factual information about

why kids should do their chores.

For ideas about how to neutralize arguing, see "What To Do When Your Kids Argue" on page 46.

MILLIONAIRE
BABIES
OR
BANKRUPT
BRATS?

Kids who manipulate by asking,

"But why?" need wise parents who repeat,

"If you don't figure that out by next week,

please let me know."

MILLIONAIRE BABIES OR BANKRUPT BRATS?

See "Put the *or* in 'I'm Bored' to Work" on page 115, "It's not fair!" on page 116, and "In a minute ... Mom!" on page 117.

Wise parents take the "chore" out of chores

*by using the **ABC** formula:*

A. *Match your expectations to your child's Ability.*

B. *Provide **Basic** training.*

C. *Learn how to gain **Cooperation**, or deliver a*

Consequence.

 See page 119.

It's easy to confuse capabilities

with expectations:

Capabilities concern the child's

ability to do something.

Expectations are about what you think

the child should be able to do.

MILLIONAIRE BABIES OR BANKRUPT BRATS?

For a list of age-appropriate chores, see page 122.

Without saying a word, we constantly

show our kids what we believe they can be.

They tend to either live up to our

highest expectations, or

live down to our greatest fears.

MILLIONAIRE BABIES OR BANKRUPT BRATS?

See "Will they ever be able to do their own laundry?"
on page 127.

Have your children work side-by-side with you. When you model your capabilities, children have opportunities to develop their own.

See the story of Megan in "A Wink at the Sink" on page 130.

MILLIONAIRE
BABIES
OR
BANKRUPT
BRATS?

It's much easier to temper

the enthusiasm of a four-year-old

than to breathe life into

a reluctant fourteen-year-old.

See "Catch 'em If You Can ... When They're Young" on page 132.

Praising kids excessively—for nothing and for everything—creates future adults who feel both fragile and entitled.

MILLIONAIRE
BABIES
OR
BANKRUPT
BRATS?

For more information about the difference between encouragement and praise, and how it affects a child's self-concept, see "Pop Quiz" on page 136.

While many people have

plenty of potential, mortgage companies

never accept it as payment.

MILLIONAIRE BABIES OR BANKRUPT BRATS?

See "Five Steps to Training Success" on page 133.

Kids should not be treated as honored houseguests in their own home.

When kids say, "Mary's mom doesn't make her do chores," wise parents smile and say, "Well that's really sad for Mary. Aren't you glad I love you enough to expect more of you?"

MILLIONAIRE BABIES OR BANKRUPT BRATS?

See the story of how one parent effectively handled the problem of incomplete chores in "How many times do I have to tell you … ?" on page 139.

Wise parents know that kids

will use guilt only if it works.

And wise parents never allow guilt

to guide their parenting.

MILLIONAIRE BABIES OR BANKRUPT BRATS?

See "Three Traps to Avoid with Kids' Excuses" on page 38, and "A Tisket a Tasket" on page 111.

Wise parents don't fear that their kids

may get angry at them.

They understand that the anger is about

not being able to control the parent,

rather than about hating the parent.

MILLIONAIRE BABIES OR BANKRUPT BRATS?

See "Lessons with Leverage" on page 145.

Never expect that giving concessions

will bring gratitude.

See "Teach an Attitude of Gratitude" on page 144.

Anger and frustration feed misbehavior.

Wise parents understand that sadness,

or empathy, is a much better teacher

than anger.

For how to use sadness instead of frustration as the teacher, see "The Core of Love and Logic: Empathy" on page 44.

When kids misbehave, wise parents

wait until they have a solid plan

before calmly delivering a heavy dose

of empathy along with

the consequence.

For an example, see "Earning Energy Back: The Energy Drain Technique" on page 53.

Wise parents can handle resistance

to doing chores with,

"No problem. I'll take care of it."

The child later finds

that they are paying someone else

to do those chores.

See the story of Emily in "Money Back Guarantee Options" on page 41.

When a child rolls their eyes

at a consequence and says,

"I don't care if you do that," wise parents

enthusiastically respond with,

"Oh thank goodness! Now we are

both happy."

MILLIONAIRE
BABIES
OR
BANKRUPT
BRATS?

For ideas about how to motivate a reluctant helper, see "Eight Steps to Motivate the Unmotivated" on page 148.

Chores are so important to

life-long success that wise parents

win this battle at all costs—

for the sake of themselves

and their children.

MILLIONAIRE
BABIES
OR
BANKRUPT
BRATS?

See "Paybacks are Heavenly!" on page 152, and "Quick ABC
Reference Guide to Contributions" on page 153.

For children to develop

internal limits,

they first need their parents to set

external ones.

MILLIONAIRE BABIES OR BANKRUPT BRATS?

For ideas, see "Mind over Money? Prioritizing Our Wants" on page 171.

Wise parents teach their children

the difference between needs and wants.

Delayed gratification is vital preparation

for a successful adult life.

See "Delayed Gratification Games" on page 172.

Wise parents who don't set limits

on their young children's "wants"

see the terrible two's multiply exponentially

during the teenage years.

MILLIONAIRE
BABIES
OR
BANKRUPT
BRATS?

See "Needs vs. Wants Starts Early" on page 159.

Kids who learn the difference

between needs and wants when young

avoid the grief and pain of

learning it later as adults.

MILLIONAIRE BABIES OR BANKRUPT BRATS?

For a fun way to introduce the difference between needs and wants to your children, see "An Introduction" on page 161.

Kids want so much more

than they really need.

But what they really need the most,

money can't buy.

MILLIONAIRE BABIES OR BANKRUPT BRATS?

For ways to teach kids the reality between their needs and their wants, see the story of Krissy in "Crossing the Double Line" on page 166.

Parents who use "You will" statements,

lose control.

Parents who use "I will" statements,

gain control.

For a look at how to effectively use an "I will" statement, see the story of Connor in "Waste Not, Want Not?" on page 156.

Kids who are taught to delay

gratification now,

learn to avoid the temptation of

instant gratification later.

For suggestions about how to use real life experiences to teach delayed gratification, see "The 48-Hour Test: Good Buy or Good Bye?" on page 168.

Give a kid a dollar, feed him for a day.

Teach a kid how to manage a dollar,

feed him for a lifetime.

MILLIONAIRE BABIES OR BANKRUPT BRATS?

For an introduction to the "Six Steps to Raising Fiscally Fit Kids," see page 179.

If you want to discover

what people truly value,

just notice where

they spend their money.

MILLIONAIRE
BABIES
OR
BANKRUPT
BRATS?

For how to say 'No' based on your values, see "The Family Values 'No'" on page 211.

Wise parents are careful not
to addict their kids to a lifestyle
they won't be able to afford
as adults.

See "My Parents' Money: MPM Rules!" on page 182.

Kids learn the most about

using money wisely when we allow them

to feel the consequences of

using it unwisely.

MILLIONAIRE
BABIES
OR
BANKRUPT
BRATS?

For several ways to set spending limits with your children, see
"When Kids Buy—Freedom, Not License" on page 184.

Regardless of a kid's age,

the best approach to setting spending limits

is a gradual one

based on responsible money use.

MILLIONAIRE
BABIES
OR
BANKRUPT
BRATS?

For guidance about how much money to give kids, see "Common Cents Approaches" on page 188.

Wise parents let their kids know

that any purchases related to safety and

well-being will be monitored

for quality assurance.

MILLIONAIRE BABIES OR BANKRUPT BRATS?

See "Taking the Slip out of the Spending Slope" on page 190.

Saying "No" to a $200 pair of sneakers

does not constitute child abuse.

MILLIONAIRE BABIES OR BANKRUPT BRATS?

For ideas about what to do when you and your child have different ideas about what to buy, see "The Luxury Tax Factor" on page 192.

Wise parents avoid unauthorized spending

by setting clear expectations,

and then holding their kids accountable

for any misuse.

MILLIONAIRE
BABIES
OR
BANKRUPT
BRATS?

For guidelines about what to do when kids abuse their spending privileges, see "Unauthorized Spending" on page 194.

People who stick to a spending plan

are free to spend their money.

People who don't stick to the plan

find that they eventually have little or no

money left to spend.

For your kid's first lesson in supply and demand, see "Budget Basics: The Planning Approach" on page 196.

MILLIONAIRE
BABIES
OR
BANKRUPT
BRATS?

There is nothing better than knowing

ways to set limits with kids,

unless…

it's knowing how to effectively enforce

those limits.

MILLIONAIRE BABIES OR BANKRUPT BRATS?

See the story of Adam in "Allowance Blues: The No-Planning Approach" on page 206.

A wise person said, "Always make the mistake with the money in your own pocket, not in someone else's."

When parents agree to share the cost of something with their child, they hold them accountable—in advance—for their share.

For ideas about joint custody of costs, see "Test Before You Invest" on page 209.

MILLIONAIRE BABIES OR BANKRUPT BRATS?

Wise parents know that saying "No" to

their children is a way to say,

"Yes! I love you enough to set limits."

For common issues parents face when saying "No" to their kids, see "When No One Buys It" on page 210.

*Parents who support each other's decisions
about what to buy their children
reduce the chances their kids will try to
"divide and conquer" to get their way.*

For what to do when parents disagree, see "When One Says 'No' and the Other Says 'Yes,'" on page 213.

Wise parents teach their children

that money doesn't buy happiness

by showing them that

the most important things in life

are not "things."

MILLIONAIRE
BABIES
OR
BANKRUPT
BRATS?

See "Money and the Happiness Factor" on page 215.

If we judge others by what they own

instead of who they are,

we raise children who confuse

net-worth with self-worth.

For guidelines about the most meaningful purchases, see "Parent Purchases" on page 214.

MILLIONAIRE
BABIES
OR
BANKRUPT
BRATS?

Kids learn to say "No" to spending

by seeing us say "No" to ourselves ...

and to them.

MILLIONAIRE BABIES OR BANKRUPT BRATS?

For three common ways adults can model more effective financial decision making, see "What We Tell Our Children" on page 219.

For overspending or underspending,

the solution is the same:

Give your kids the money you would

normally spend for their needs and let them

practice being the buyer.

MILLIONAIRE BABIES OR BANKRUPT BRATS?

For ideas about putting this principle into practice see "Do You Have an Overspender or an Underspender?" on page 222.

Wise grandparents "spoil" their grandchildren by giving them lots of time instead of lots of money.

MILLIONAIRE
BABIES
OR
BANKRUPT
BRATS?

See "How to Spoil Your Grandchildren Without Ruining Them" on page 225.

Family members who give your children

too much stuff need the same

Love and Logic limit-setting we provide

for our children.

MILLIONAIRE BABIES OR BANKRUPT BRATS?

For more ideas about how to handle conflicts, see "Intergenerational Differences" on page 226.

It's amazing how quickly

kids clean up their toys when parents say,

"You may keep the toys you pick up."

MILLIONAIRE BABIES OR BANKRUPT BRATS?

For ways to handle the "too many toys syndrome," see "Storage or Standing Room Only?" on page 217.

Failure to teach kids how to

live within their means

threatens the quality of their life

as adults.

See "Eight Ways to Say 'No' to 'Buy-Buy'" on page 229.

MILLIONAIRE
BABIES
OR
BANKRUPT
BRATS?

Wise parents remember two things when

teaching their kids to save:

the presence of choice

and the absence of rescue.

MILLIONAIRE
BABIES
OR
BANKRUPT
BRATS?

See "Using Life's Little Emergencies to Teach" on page 236.

Kids who learn how to save when young

won't need to be saved

from poor money management

when they are older.

MILLIONAIRE BABIES OR BANKRUPT BRATS?

For two approaches to inspiring your children to save, see "By Hook or Book" on page 234.

Real life experiences of, "I want a _____

but I spent my money already," are the

financial wedgies that teach kids to save

by allowing them the experience

of running out of money.

MILLIONAIRE
BABIES
OR
BANKRUPT
BRATS?

See the story "Throwing the Book at Travis" on page 233.

Wise parents give their kids lots of

opportunities to save money

by not buying them

everything they want.

MILLIONAIRE
BABIES
OR
BANKRUPT
BRATS?

See "Toy du Jour Desires: Keeping Kids Interested in Saving" on page 247, and "Five Kid-Sized Reasons to Save Money" on page 250.

Smart parents know how to set limits

by agreeing with their kids:

"I agree! Those sneakers are great.

I'll contribute 20 percent. Won't it be great

when you've saved enough money

to cover the rest?"

MILLIONAIRE BABIES OR BANKRUPT BRATS?

See "Luxury Tax Factor: What Our Children Want" on page 193.

Learning how to save for

the things we want is the first step

to knowing we can obtain them.

See "Six Keys to Incentive-Style Saving" on page 239, and
"When should I open a savings account for my child?"
on page 244.

Wise parents can test the strength

of their child's desire for something

by saying,

"Feel free to spend your own money for that."

MILLIONAIRE BABIES OR BANKRUPT BRATS?

For how to guide kids to turn their potential desires into decisions, see "Five Steps to Wishing Well" on page 253.

Parents who teach their kids

how to prioritize their wishes

raise kids who have plenty of opportunities

to discover if their wishes match

their financial realities.

MILLIONAIRE BABIES OR BANKRUPT BRATS?

For ideas about how to use a wish list, see "Dreams and Schemes: The Real Cost of a Pet" on page 257.

A kid with a savings plan

takes the monkey off the parent's back

because the plan determines the child's

financial reality, not you.

MILLIONAIRE BABIES OR BANKRUPT BRATS? For ideas about how to handle savings withdrawals, see "The Case for Financial Planning" on page 260.

Kids who frequently practice

borrowing and repaying loans when young

rarely experience bankruptcy

as adults.

See "Bottom Line: Be a Home That Loans" on page 300.

Wise parents remember that

it's not a loan if there is

no guarantee of repayment.

MILLIONAIRE BABIES OR BANKRUPT BRATS?

See "The Love and Logic of Loans: Hero or Zero?" on page 264.

Love and Logic parents know that rescuing kids by loaning them money is rarely a good idea.

Rescue teaches entitlement.

Repayment teaches character.

For a look at one dad's decision to loan money or not, see the story of Brittany in "A Gift or a Loan?" on page 264.

A loan request and a solid

repayment plan should originate from

the child, not the parent.

MILLIONAIRE
BABIES
OR
BANKRUPT
BRATS?

For guidelines and a list of great loan opportunities for kids,
see "When to Loan" on page 268.

Wise parents do not extend new loans

until outstanding loans have been

repaid in full.

For tips to determine age-appropriate loans, see "Types of Loans" on page 272.

Wise parents keep the amount of the loan

relative to their child's age, income

and ability to repay.

MILLIONAIRE
BABIES
OR
BANKRUPT
BRATS?

For guidelines about how much to loan, see "Kid-Sized Loans"
on page 275.

The basic qualifier for kids

is the same for adults:

Don't lend more than you will get back!

Don't borrow more than you can pay back!

MILLIONAIRE BABIES OR BANKRUPT BRATS?

For a variety of ways to provide financial assistance while teaching accountability, see "To Match, Limit, or Grant?" on page 276.

Matching funds are like riding a
tandem bike. They have a built-in test
that measures the determination
to keep in balance with the incentive
to keep on pedaling.

MILLIONAIRE
BABIES
OR
BANKRUPT
BRATS?

See "Matching Funds" on page 277 for ratio ideas, and "Test Before You Invest" on page 209.

Wise parents secure a note from their kids,

such as a signed cashier's receipt,

a written I.O.U., or a promissory note,

as the perfect preparation for adult loans.

MILLIONAIRE BABIES OR BANKRUPT BRATS?

For tips about how to set up a repayment plan, see "Making a Note: After the Quote" on page 280.

Wise parents teach their children

the power of their signature

and what honoring the agreement

to "sign here" really means.

See "'X' Marks the Spot" on page 283.

MILLIONAIRE
BABIES
OR
BANKRUPT
BRATS?

No pay, no play. No fund, no fun.

Until the child repays the loan in full,

wise parents keep their kid's toys

unopened in the box as collateral.

MILLIONAIRE
BABIES
OR
BANKRUPT
BRATS?

For ideas about payback policies, see "Collecting Collateral" on page 284.

If your teen cannot be responsible

for the cost associated with owning

and operating a vehicle, then they are not

ready for the privileges and responsibilities

associated with driving a car.

MILLIONAIRE BABIES OR BANKRUPT BRATS?

See "Hormones, Wheels, and Deals" on page 293.

Kids learn faster about

the responsibility of possessions

when they are allowed to experience

the consequences of repossessions.

MILLIONAIRE
BABIES
OR
BANKRUPT
BRATS?

See "Loan Consequences: Default, Credit, and Repossession"
on page 296.

What might seem like

the wrong thing to do in the short term

is often the right thing to do

in the long term.

MILLIONAIRE BABIES OR BANKRUPT BRATS?

See "How to Ruin the Effectiveness of a Consequence"
on page 298.

Kids who experience how debt
can affect the quality of their lives
when young tend to avoid the devastating
effects of excess debt as adults.

See "The Dangers of Never Giving Loans to Kids" on page 267.

Wise parents know

that it is best for kids to learn how to go

"first class" as a result of their own efforts

and their own money.

MILLIONAIRE
BABIES
OR
BANKRUPT
BRATS?

For how to give kids firsthand opportunities to earn money, see "An Education in Earning" on page 304.

If your kids are not earning

the grades they get, the car they drive,

the things they want,

and the privileges you give them,

their economic future is at risk.

MILLIONAIRE BABIES OR BANKRUPT BRATS?

See "Earn Local, Think Global" on page 306.

Kids who practice doing jobs at home

are better prepared than their peers

for doing jobs in the workplace.

See "First Day on the Job" on page 307, and for a list of age-appropriate jobs at home, see page 309.

For jobs that are done together

for the good of the whole family,

payment comes in the form of

connection, not coins.

MILLIONAIRE
BABIES
OR
BANKRUPT
BRATS?

For guidelines about family jobs, see page 312.

When determining whether or not

to pay kids for completed jobs,

wise parents ask themselves:

"Would my child's future spouse pay them

to do what I'm asking?"

MILLIONAIRE BABIES OR BANKRUPT BRATS?

See "Job or Contribution? The Difference a Dollar Makes" on page 313, and sample "Jobs vs. Contributions" lists on page 315.

A job list collects dust very quickly

unless adults keep their wallets closed.

Wise parents know that a job list

is the "perfect referral" in the land of

materialistic desires.

MILLIONAIRE
BABIES
OR
BANKRUPT
BRATS?

For a look at how one parent introduced a job list to his two sons, and their reactions, see the story of Mason and Blake in "Introducing a Job List" on page 317.

Children whose parents teach them to work

and achieve are much more likely to inherit

the keys to the kingdom.

They have an advantage over kids

whose parents allow them to grow up

waiting for the keys to be handed to them.

MILLIONAIRE
BABIES
OR
BANKRUPT
BRATS?

For how to develop ethics and skills around work, see "Learning to Earn" on page 319.

Wise parents never

pay their kids to do a job

when the neighbor kids

are willing to do it better...

and for less.

MILLIONAIRE BABIES OR BANKRUPT BRATS?

See "How Much to Pay?" on page 322, and "Mason Negotiates for a Car Wash" on page 325.

When kids say, "But, it's only $20.00"

or "They're only $99.95,"

they're really saying,

"I need a lot more experience doing without

some of the things I want."

MILLIONAIRE BABIES OR BANKRUPT BRATS?

See the story of Sydney in "Easy Money: Turning Depreciation into Appreciation" on page 330.

When children start their own

business ventures, wise parents never

work harder than their children.

MILLIONAIRE BABIES OR BANKRUPT BRATS? For ideas about guiding young entrepreneurs, see "Jobs: Self-Employment" on page 334, and "Too big for your britches!" on page 255.

Losing a low-paying job

due to irresponsibility at age fifteen

might be the experience

that teaches how to

keep a higher-paying job later in life.

MILLIONAIRE
BABIES
OR
BANKRUPT
BRATS?

For a look at employing your kids in a family-owned business, see page 343.

Wise parents offer guidance

while keeping responsibility

for the problems their children create

where it belongs:

squarely on their children's shoulders.

For how to hand the problem back to the child, see "Accountability 101" on page 55.

Wise parents never try to convince kids

that their decisions are fair.

For different viewpoints about whether teens should work while attending school, see "Employment and Teens" on page 339.

MILLIONAIRE
BABIES
OR
BANKRUPT
BRATS?

Wise parents know that arguments

are not requests to hear parental wisdom.

Instead they are designed to

weaken a parent's resolve.

For ideas about how to avoid battles over teen spending, see "Allowance, Earnings, and Paychecks" on page 350. See also "What to Do When Your Kids Argue" on page 46.

Wise parents know that

it is not in their kid's best interest

to pay them for good grades.

MILLIONAIRE
BABIES
OR
BANKRUPT
BRATS?

For a look at how rewards can become bribes, see "Pay for Grades?" on page 355.

Wise parents know that it is not in

their kid's best interest

to tie driving privileges to good grades.

MILLIONAIRE BABIES OR BANKRUPT BRATS?

For a dangerous assumption about teen driving and safety, see "No B's, No Keys?" on page 357.

When it comes to kids and earning,

the issue is less about

the amount of money earned

and more about opportunities to experience

the value and meaning of doing work.

MILLIONAIRE
BABIES
OR
BANKRUPT
BRATS?

For ideas about giving kids opportunities to experience the meaning of effort, see "What about Blase' Blake?" on page 358.

Parents who satisfy their child's

every materialistic whim create

kids who never have a reason to yearn,

learn, and earn on their own.

See "The World's Best Job Benefit Package" on page 362.

MILLIONAIRE
BABIES
OR
BANKRUPT
BRATS?

Wise parents help their children

connect the financial dots

between education and earnings

so that they can afford the lifestyle

of their own choosing.

MILLIONAIRE
BABIES
OR
BANKRUPT
BRATS?

For ideas about teaching kids what buying something with their own money really means, see "A Wage Against Reality" on page 344.

While the value of the dollar may change,

the value of learning how to

manage a dollar wisely will not.

MILLIONAIRE
BABIES
OR
BANKRUPT
BRATS?

For ideas about getting kids interested in investing, see "A Zest to Invest" on page 366.

*Wise parents use the opportunity
to introduce "financial planning" on
the first day their child wants
two or more things that the parent is
unwilling to purchase.*

See "Egads! Fifteen Wishes?" on page 251.

Your children are on the road to financial

independence when they repeatedly

purchase things, with their own money,

that their peers cannot.

For an introduction to goal setting, see the story of Maria in "Taking Stock" on page 376.

Kids who live through little recessions

when young can avoid the big recessions

as adults.

MILLIONAIRE
BABIES
OR
BANKRUPT
BRATS?

For a look at how one mom handled this lesson, see the story of Josh in "In Case of Emergency" on page 367.

Wise investors never invest in anything

when they don't have a say

in the rules.

MILLIONAIRE BABIES OR BANKRUPT BRATS?

For the story of how one grandparent introduced his grand-children to the world of investing, see "Grandpa's Money Garden" on page 380.

While kids may not have many

financial assets to capitalize on,

they have one that's

much bigger than their parents'—

the dividends of time.

See "Turning Star Bucks into Big Bucks: The Half Million Dollar Mocha" on page 399, and "Win-Win: The Magic of Compound Interest" on page 246.

To prevent struggles over inherited money,

wise parents and grandparents

are clear about their expectations

so that their heirs can be clear

about their own.

MILLIONAIRE BABIES OR BANKRUPT BRATS?

See "Inheritance: Squandering and Squabbling" on page 396.

Wise parents teach their children

how to invest in themselves

so that they can become their own CEO:

Contribute Early and Often.

MILLIONAIRE
BABIES
OR
BANKRUPT
BRATS?

See the story of Brent in "So You Want to Be a Millionaire?" on page 384, and "Investing in the Next Generation" on page 404.

Kids who are required to contribute

to their family life at home

are more likely to contribute to

their communities as adults.

MILLIONAIRE BABIES OR BANKRUPT BRATS?

See "A Heritage of Helping" on page 421.

Kids are more willing to share

when they have a say

in choosing the cause.

MILLIONAIRE
BABIES
OR
BANKRUPT
BRATS?

For ideas about connecting the child to the charitable cause,
see "Sharing How-To's" on page 414.

The issue is not the amount of the donation.

The issue is about teaching kids

how to share with others

who are less fortunate.

MILLIONAIRE BABIES OR BANKRUPT BRATS?

For how to offer kids choices about sharing, see "The Three T's: Time, Talent, or Tithe" on page 419.

Wise parents never waste words

trying to talk their kids into caring.

For ideas about how to teach kids the value of sharing, see the story of Jill in "Care to Share?" on page 406.

Parents who delay consequences

have the immediate luxury of doing

discipline without breaking a sweat.

MILLIONAIRE BABIES OR BANKRUPT BRATS?

For a look at how one parent used the delayed consequence, see "Jill Will or Jill the Pill?" on page 409. See also "It Pays to Delay: The Delayed Consequence" on page 52.

Wise parents redirect their teen's angst and

their desire to be free and independent—

into helping those in need be

more free and independent.

MILLIONAIRE
BABIES
OR
BANKRUPT
BRATS?

See "Sharing: An Antidote for the Troubled or Entitled Teen" on
page 426.

Kids who learn the meaning

of being part of a team effort in childhood

grow up understanding how team effort

contributes to success as adults.

MILLIONAIRE BABIES OR BANKRUPT BRATS?

For a look at how to involve the whole family in a charitable project, see "Making a Family Match" on page 422.

Wise parents never force sharing.

Mandates rarely come from the heart.

MILLIONAIRE
BABIES
OR
BANKRUPT
BRATS?

For advice concerning young children, see "When Sharing Is Not a Good Idea" on page 413.

The measure of a person's life

is more about what we can give

than what we can get.

For ideas about ways to introduce age-appropriate sharing, see "Charity Begins at Home" on page 425.

Wise parents remember that their kids

may well be the ones

to manage their future finances and

pick their retirement home.

MILLIONAIRE BABIES OR BANKRUPT BRATS?

For a look at how parents can underwrite their own financial future, see "Financial Prevention, Not Tension" on page 430.

In the end …

While life holds no guarantees,

taking good care of our money,

and teaching our children well,

raises the odds that our money,

and our children,

will take good care of us.

About the Author

Jim Fay's background includes thirty-one years as a teacher and administrator, twenty-four years as a professional consultant and public speaker, and many years as a parent of three children. He serves both nationally and internationally as a consultant to schools, parent organizations, and the U.S. military. Jim believes his major accomplishment in life is the development (along with Foster W. Cline, M.D.) of a unique philosophy of practical techniques for enhancing communication between children and adults, known as Love and Logic. Jim has taken complex problems and broken them down into simple, easy-to-use concepts and techniques that can be understood and used by anyone. Hundreds of thousands of people have expressed how Love and Logic has enhanced their relationships with their children. Jim is one of America's most sought-after presenters in the area of parenting and school discipline. His practical techniques are revolutionizing the way parents and professionals are looking at how we deal with children; how we help them to become responsible, thinking people; and how we help them enhance their own self-concepts.

About the Author

Kristan Leatherman, M.S. is an educational consultant, national speaker, and family life counselor with over twenty years of experience working with parents, children, and educators. She is known for her commitment to raising self-reliant, responsible children, as well as her passion for supporting adults with practical and effective ideas that build and sustain positive relationships with children and students.

Kristan presents seminars on a variety of topics to schools, colleges, and community and youth service organizations at local, regional, and national conferences from coast to coast. She has written numerous articles and is the coauthor (with Jim Fay) of *Millionaire Babies or Bankrupt Brats? Love and Logic Solutions to Teaching Kids About Money.*

Kristan is the founder of the Millionaire Babies Project, an initiative that uses her books, seminars, private consultations, and personal experience to jumpstart America's need to teach our children personal and financial responsibility.

To learn more about Kristan and her services, contact:
www.RaisingMillionaireBabies.com
kristanleatherman@sbcglobal.net
530-879-9126

Love and Logic Seminars

Jim and Kristan are available to present Love and Logic seminars, for both parents and educators, in many cities throughout the year.

For more information, contact the Speaker Appearance Coordinator at 1-800-338-4065, or visit www.loveandlogic.com